Ted Naifeh's

PRINCESS UGG

Written and Illustrated by
TED NAIFEH

Colored and Lettered by
WARREN WUCINICH

Watercolor Sequences by
TED NAIFEH

‡

Princess Ugg Volume 2 Cover Colored by
WARREN WUCINICH

Edited by
ROBIN HERRERA

Designed by
JASON STOREY

Published by Oni Press, Inc.
***Joe Nozemack**, publisher*
***James Lucas Jones**, editor in chief*
***Cheyenne Allott**, director of sales*
***Fred Reckling**, director of publicity*
***Troy Look**, production manager*
***Hilary Thompson**, graphic designer*
***Jared Jones**, production assistant*
***Charlie Chu**, senior editor*
***Robin Herrera**, editor*
***Ari Yarwood**, associate editor*
***Brad Rooks**, inventory coordinator*
***Jung Lee**, office assistant*

Originally published as issues 5-8 of the Oni Press comic series *Princess Ugg*.

Princess Ugg Volume 2, August 2015. Published by Oni Press, Inc.
1305 SE Martin Luther King, Jr. Blvd., Suite A, Portland, OR 97214.

Oni Press, Inc.
1305 SE Martin Luther King, Jr. Blvd.
Suite A
Portland, OR 97214

www.onipress.com
facebook.com/onipress · twitter.com/onipress · onipress.tumblr.com

tednaifeh.com · warrenwucinich.carbonmade.com

First Edition: August 2015
ISBN 978-1-62010-215-2 · eISBN 978-1-62010-216-9

1 3 5 7 9 10 8 6 4 2

Library of Congress Control Number: 2014953740

Printed in China.

chapter 5

PHOE?
DES?
ARE YOU THERE?
KEEP IT DOWN!

ONE WOULD THINK YOU'D NEVER DONE THIS BEFORE.
WHO'S TO HEAR US OUT HERE? IT'S SNEAKING PAST MY ROOMMATE THAT PROVED...

...DIFFICULT...

I WONDERED WHY YOU WEREN'T SNORING.
'TWAS SOME O' YER EXTRA CUSHIONS.
PHOENICIA'S IDEA.

HOW RESOURCEFUL.
YOU MAY KEEP THEM IF YOU LIKE. OR BURN THEM.

I JUST HOPE SOMEONE TOLD HER TO KEEP HER MOUTH SHUT ABOUT THIS.

The Rollicking Dragon

FOR GOODNESS' SAKE, JULIE. CAN'T YOU TRY BEING NICE FOR ONCE?

WHAT'S THIS? DO YOU LOVELY YOUNG LADIES REQUIRE A CHAPERONE?

YOU REMEMBER THE LADS.
ROSELYN, SOME WINE FOR THE NEWCOMERS.
BUDGE UP, LADS. MAKE SOME ROOM.

LIEUTENANT, THIS IS OUR FRIEND, ÜLGA.
YOU DON'T LOOK LIKE A PRINCESS.

SHE'S NOT. NONE OF THEM ARE. REMEMBER, KIT?

OH YES. I FORGOT.
sigh
HAVE SOME MORE ALE, LIEUTENANT.

CAN YOU DO THAT AGAIN?

AYE, IF SOMEONE GI' ME ANOTHER WEE DRINKIE.

IS IT TRUE THE WOMEN OF THE GRIMMERIANS ARE AS STRONG AS THE MEN?

DEPENDS ON WHICH MEN YEH MEAN.

HOW 'BOUT THIS ONE, EH, GIRLY?

NOW JACK, DON'T BE A LOUT.
IT'S JUST GOOD FUN, CAPTAIN.
WHAT AM I SUPPOSED TEH DO WI' THAT?

IT'S ARM WRESTLING. IF I PUSH YOUR ARM TO THE TABLE, I WIN.
ONE, TWO...

...THREE.
...UH...

I THOUGHT YOU COULD BEAT ANYONE, JACK.
AN' HOW DO I WIN?
THE SAME WAY.

LIKE THIS?
EXACTLY.
EARGH!
THUNK

YOU'LL HAVE TO EXCUSE OUR COMPANION. SHE WASN'T PROPERLY BROUGHT UP.
DON'T BE SILLY. SHE'S THE LIFE OF THE PARTY.

AND SHE SAVED JULIFER'S BACON THIS AFTERNOON.
THREE CHEERS FOR PRINCESS UGG!

HIP HIP HURRAH!
HIP HIP HURRAH!

HIP HIP HURRAH!

I SAW YEH ON THE FIELD TODAY, BOYO. NO' TOO BAD FOR A LOWLANDER.
THANKS. I LIKE TO THINK I CAN HOLD MY OWN.

RECKON SO. BUT IF YEH EVER NEEDED HELP...
ERR...
THE LASSIES ARE RIGHT, YEH REALLY ARE A BONNY LAD.
WELL, THANK-

SOMETHIN' WRONG?

EH, ÜLGA, THAT'S NOT... ER...

WHAT THE CAPTAIN MEANS TO SAY IS, THAT'S NOT HOW A LADY CONDUCTS HERSELF.

I DINNAE UNDERSTAND. YEH ALL BEEN FLIRTIN' WITH THEM LADS ALL NIGHT.

Time, the great devourer, consumed the winter, and iron-willed Ülga pursued her course.

EXCELLENT WORK, YOUR HIGHNESS.
Whatever else might be said of my lord's progeny, once she sets herself a task...
NOT WHOLLY UNACCEPTABLE. I'M GLAD SOMETHING HAS RUBBED OFF AT LAST.
...no matter how arduous or arcane...
WELL DONE, PRINCESS. YOU'VE IMPROVED ENORMOUSLY.
...she will not rest until she's accomplished it.
THE HISTOREY OF QUEEN FRIDRIKA OF GRIMMERIA
SO, SHE'S NO' COMIN' BACK?
Nay, O King.
THE GIANTS WILLNAE WAIT FOR SPRING, I THINK.

AN' THIS TIME, THERE'LL BE NAE RETREAT. THEY'LL BATTLE TEH THE DEATH, EVERY MOTHER'S SON O' 'EM.
WE CANNAE WAIT MUCH LONGER FOR THIS "BETTER WAY" SHE'S GONE TEH FETCH.

IF SHE RETURNS WI' IT, AND I'M GONE, TELL HER THIS.
YEH WAS THE BRAVEST O' ALL OF US, ME BONNY WEE BERZERKER.
I SEE THA' NOW.

I MUST SAY, ÜLGA, I HARDLY RECOGNIZE YOU.

IF, SIX MONTHS AGO, ANYONE WERE TO LOOK AT YOU AND SAY, "SHE'S GOING TO BE CHOSEN TO VISIT QUEEN ASTORIA," I'D HAVE LAUGHED IN THEIR FACE.
BUT LOOK AT YOU NOW.

IT'S TRUE. YOU LOOK AMAZING.
DO YEH REALLY THINK SO?
WITHOUT A DOUBT.

GOOD MORNING, LADIES. I HOPE YOU'RE ALL COMFORTABLE. IT'S A LONG JOURNEY.

I DON'T WANT TO HEAR ANY SILLY TALK ABOUT BANDITS. YOU'RE PROTECTED BY THE FINEST SOLDIERS IN THE WORLD.

SAVING YOUR PRESENCE, MILADY.

GOSH, THAT WAS QUITE A LOOK HE GAVE YOU.
LUCKY YOU, ÜLGA. HE'S QUITE A CATCH.
AND IT SEEMS HE'S QUITE FORGOTTEN HIS INFERIOR STATUS.

PERHAPS IT HAS SOMETHING TO DO WITH THE WAY YOU DEGRADED YOURSELF IN FRONT OF HIM.

GOODNESS, BUT YOU'VE GOTTEN GOOD AT THAT LUTE.

I CAN ALMOST PICK OUT THE TUNE.
'TIS CALLED "GREEN SLEEVES."

SHE OUGHT TO SOUND BETTER. SHE PLAYS THE THING EVERY NIGHT.
WILL YOU PLAY FOR THE QUEEN?

NO' IF I CAN AVOID IT. I'VE NAE WISH TO HUMILIATE MESELF.
NONSENSE. THAT'S WHY WE'RE GOING.
I'M GOING TO PERFORM A ROSE PETAL DANCE. THE QUEEN LOVES THE PERFORMING ARTS.

I'M GOING TO RECITE THE SUBLIME POETRY OF THE PHILOSOPHER MIKUS.

I'M GOING TO SING "THE SERPENT'S EGG." WHAT ARE YOU DOING, JULIE?

I'M RIDING.
OH? DID YOU EVER GET THAT UNICORN OFF THE ROOF?

NO, BUT ÜLGA WAS KIND ENOUGH TO LEND ME HER PONY AGAIN.
sigh
SUCH AS IT IS.

I STILL DON'T SEE WHY YOU'RE LENDING GERTA TO JULIE AGAIN. SHE'S NOT VERY GRATEFUL, IS SHE?

SHE'S BEEN HELPIN' WI' ME LUTE PLAYIN'. FAIR TRADE.

DOESN'T SEEM WORTH IT IF SHE'S JUST GOING TO BE MEAN TO YOU ALL THE TIME.

DOCTOR GAMOOSH SAYS THE FOUNDATION O' FRIENDSHIP IS MUTUAL DEPENDENCE.

BETWEEN KINGDOMS, MAYBE. I DON'T KNOW IF THAT APPLIES TO JULIFER.

AYE, WELL, I RECKON I MADE A GREAT HAMES O' THINGS. I GOT A LOT TEH MAKE UP FOR. WHO KNEW T'WERE SO MUCH EFFORT JUST BEIN' A PRINCESS?

BANDITS. AND NOT TOO FAR AWAY.
HMMM. BE ON GUARD, BUT DON'T CONCERN YOURSELF OVERLY.

THEIR NUMBERS ARE FEW. I DOUBT THEY'LL BE FOOL ENOUGH TO TAKE US ON.
CAPTAIN, ARE YEH IN THERE?

PRINCESS ÜLGA?
I, ERR, FEEL AS THOUGH WE GOT OFF ON THE WRONG FOOT, IF YEH FOLLOW ME.
I THOUGHT MEBBE WE COULD CLEAR THE AIR, START AGAIN.

CERTAINLY, BUT NOW MIGHT NOT–
DINNAE WORRY. I BEEN LEARNIN' PROPER ETTYKIT FOR LADIES, SO I KNOW IT WOULD'NAE BE PROPER–
MAL, ARE YOU COMING TO BED?

YOU DON'T KNOW WHAT YOU'RE-

-MISSING...
SO THIS IS WHAT "PROPER" MEANS.

SILLY ME, I STILL HAD IT WRONG.

YOU MUST PROMISE YOU WON'T TELL.

FINE, BUT IT'LL COST YEH.
YOU'RE BLACKMAILING ME?

LET'S JUST SAY YEH'LL FEEL MORE CONFIDENT O' ME PROMISE IF I HAD WHAT DOCTOR GAMOOSH CALLS A "VESTED INTEREST."
THAT'S WHAT YOU FOLK CALL "DIPLOMACY."

ME MISTAKE WAS THINKIN' IT WERE THE SAME AS FRIENDSHIP.

I HOPE YOU SLEPT WELL.

AYE. I WAS JUST MULLIN' OVER WHA' KIND O' FAVOR YEH MIGHT BE GOOD FOR.
I'VE BEEN THINKING ABOUT THAT MYSELF.

AND I'VE DECIDED YOU CAN TELL THE OTHERS WHATEVER YOU LIKE...

...AND SEE HOW LONG THEY STAY "FRIENDS."
YEH THINK THEY WON'T BELIEVE ME?

ALL THEY'LL KNOW FOR SURE IS THAT YOU'RE EITHER A LIAR OR A BLABBERMOUTH.
YOU STILL DON'T GET IT.

YOU CAN WEAR THAT DRESS, LEARN TO PLAY THE LUTE AND HOLD TEACUPS PROPERLY.
BUT TO ME, AND TO THIS WORLD, YOU'LL ALWAYS BE PRINCESS UGG.

IT'S NOT SOMETHING YOU CAN LEARN, ANYMORE THAN I COULD LEARN TO BE A... A BARBARIAN.

MAYBE YOU SHOULD JUST ACCEPT WHAT YOU ARE.

SHIELDS UP! ARCHERS, LET FLY YOUR ARROWS!

thunk

thunk

SLASH

thunk

thunk

WHAT HAVE WE HERE?

CRUNCH

THIS ONE'S GOT SOME FIGHT IN HER.

DON'T MAKE THIS HARDER THAN IT HAS TO BE, PRINCESS. THIS SWORD AIN'T A TOY.

IT IS THE WAY *YOU* PLAY WI' IT, YEH KNACKER!
SHUNK

SUFFERIN' TASH! WHAT KIND OF PRINCESS ARE YOU?
I'M YER WORST NIGHTMARE, BOYO!
BUT YEH CAN CALL ME PRINCESS UGG!

chapter 6

WELL, NOW IT'S MY TURN TEH TAKE YEH LADS TEH SCHOOL!

LESSON ONE!

THE WEAPON YEH DINNAE KNOW HOW TEH USE ***BELONGS TEH YER ENEMY!***

SLICE

SLASH

HACK

HO THERE, PRINCESS. HERE'S A CRASH COURSE FOR YOU.

SHWIPP

OH, YEH WANT SOME O' THIS, EH?

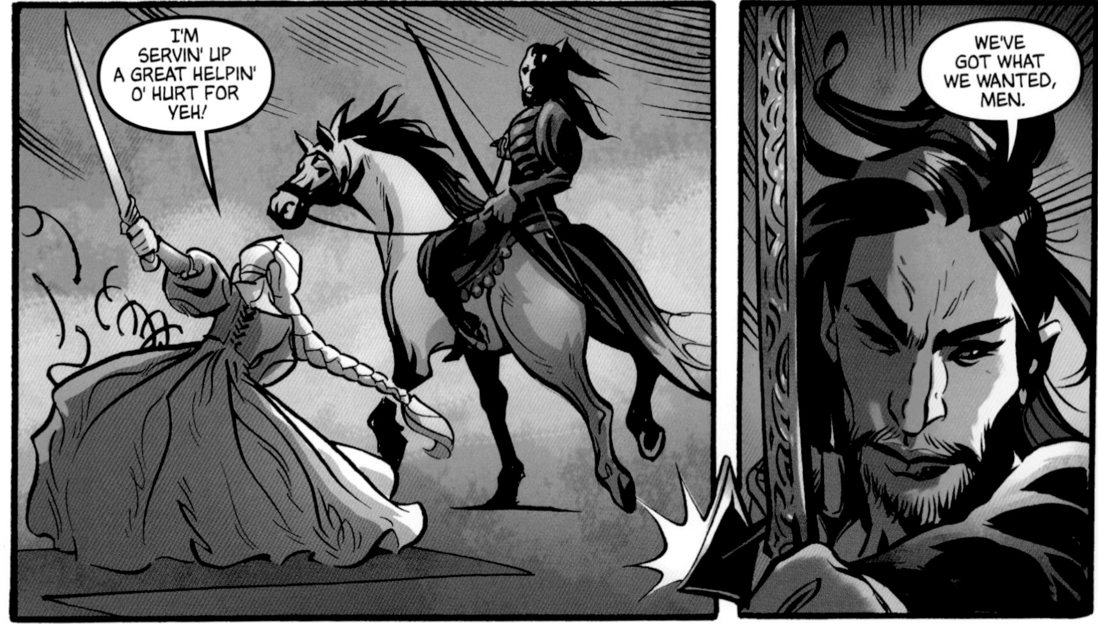
I'M SERVIN' UP A GREAT HELPIN' O' HURT FOR YEH!
WE'VE GOT WHAT WE WANTED, MEN.

thunk

LET'S RIDE!

YOU'RE SAFE. THANK GOODNESS. I THOUGHT YOU'D-
THEY'RE NAE GREAT SHAKES AT RIDIN'. WE CAN STILL CATCH 'EM.

LET THEM GO. A FEW VALUABLES AREN'T WORTH-

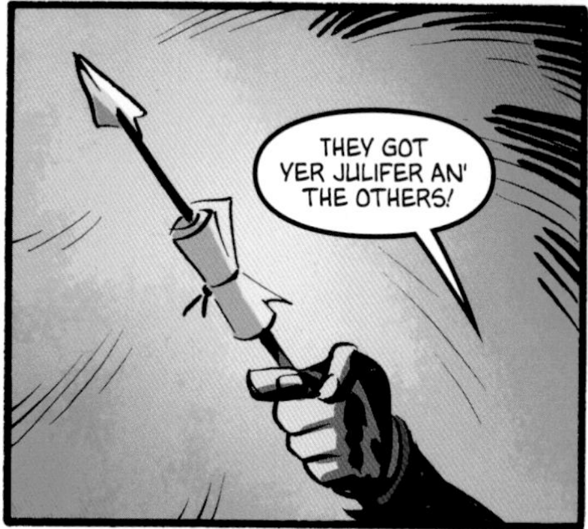
THEY GOT YER JULIFER AN' THE OTHERS!

THEY WANT A RANSOM. WE MUST RETURN TO THE CITY-
GO WHERE YEH LIKE. I'M GOIN' AFTER 'EM.
ÜLGA, HOSTAGE SITUATIONS CALL FOR CAREFUL NEGOTIATION. DIPLOMACY.

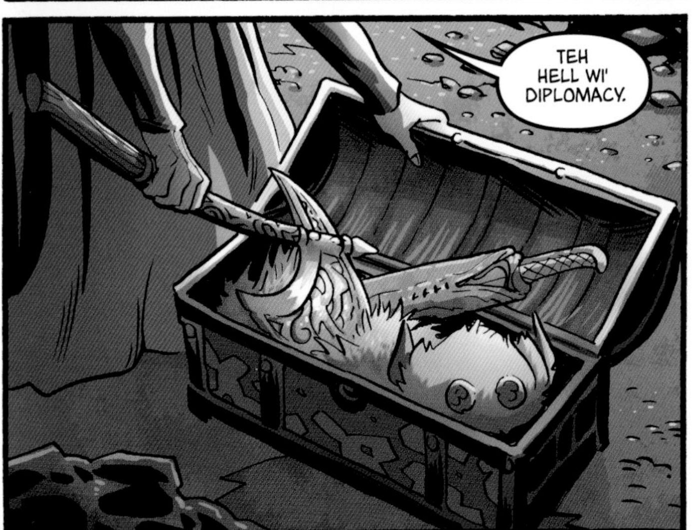
TEH HELL WI' DIPLOMACY.

GERTA! TEH ME!
STOP! LISTEN TO ME!

THIS ISN'T A MOUNTAIN BATTLE.
TO THESE MEN, IT'S A BUSINESS TRANSACTION. IF WE HANDLE IT LIKE CIVILIZED PEOPLE, NO ONE WILL GET HURT.
SURE ABOUT THAT, ARE YEH?
ABSOLUTELY!

SURE ENOUGH TEH BET THEIR LIVES ON IT?
...

NO.

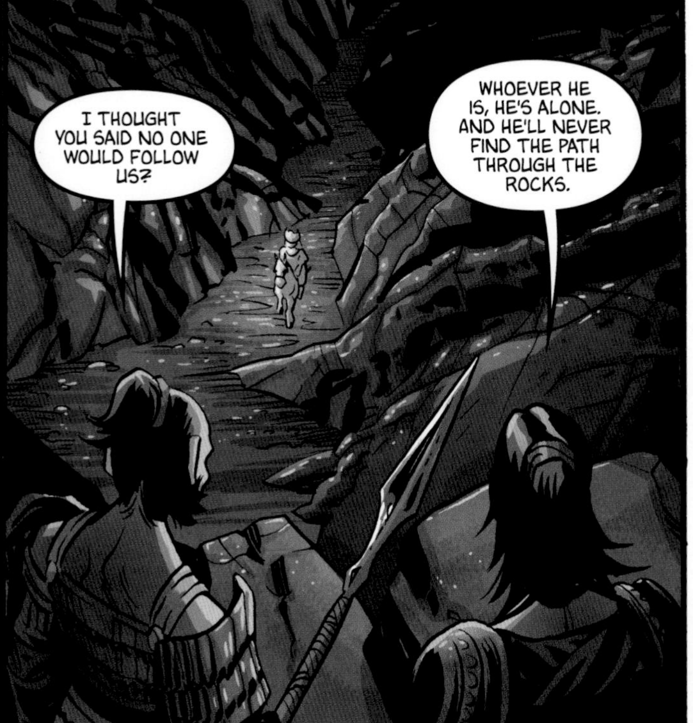
I THOUGHT YOU SAID NO ONE WOULD FOLLOW US?
WHOEVER HE IS, HE'S ALONE. AND HE'LL NEVER FIND THE PATH THROUGH THE ROCKS.

I'M GOING TO MAKE SURE OUR GUESTS ARE COMFORTABLE.

PLEASE DON'T HURT US!
MY FATHER IS VERY POWERFUL! IF YOU TOUCH US–
DON'T LET YOUR FEVERISH LITTLE IMAGINATIONS RUN AWAY WITH YOU.

I'M A MAN OF THE WORLD. I KNOW THE VALUE OF A PRINCESS ISN'T IN HER LIFE, BUT HER VIRTUE.
AND IF MY PRICE IS MET, YOU KEEP BOTH.
FROM THE SPOILS. NOT BAD. SEE ANYTHING OF OUR LONE HERO?
TRAIL'S CLEAR. HE'S PROBABLY AT THE BOTTOM OF A GORGE BY NOW.

SHIKRA! COME QUICK!
WHAT IS IT, MAN?

I... I DON'T KNOW!

IT'S IMPOSSIBLE. WHO COULD HAVE FOUND US?
THE HOSTAGES!

ÜLGA! HOW DID YOU FIND US IN THIS LABYRINTH?
TWISTED ONE O' THEM KNACKERS' FINGERS TILL HE FOUND HIS TONGUE.

CHUNK
THIS DIPLOMACY BUSINESS IS EASY ONCE YEH GET THE HANG O' IT.
STAY CLOSE.
I'M NOT GOING ANYWHERE.

ARE YOU INSANE?
CAPTAIN MALICK WILL COME, THEY'LL PAY A RANSOM, AND THAT WILL BE THAT.

PRINCESS UGG THERE IS GOING TO GET YOU KILLED.

I'LL TAKE MY CHANCES. LEAD ON, ÜLGA.

DES, STAY BEHIND ME. YOU TWO, WATCH YER BACKS.
IF ANY KNACKER COMES UP BEHIND US, SCREAM YER HEADS OFF.

I DON'T SEE ANYONE.
ME NEITHER.

THAT'S FAR ENOUGH. THROW DOWN YOUR WEAPONS OR WE LET FLY OUR ARROWS.

GET BACK!
KLIK
KLAK
WE GIVE UP! DON'T HURT US!

GOOD. NOW THROW DOWN YOUR WEAPONS.

AND WE CAN TALK LIKE CIVILIZED PEOPLE.

THUNK
RAAAAAAAAAAAAA
GREAT YOG!
I NEVER IMAGINED...
IS SHE HUMAN?

THAT'S NO PRINCESS! SHE'S A *DEMON*.
INDEED.
MAGNIFICENT, ISN'T SHE?

RAAAAAWWWRRR!?!

VERY WELL, WE'LL DO IT YOUR WAY.
GRRR!

SURRENDER, OR YOUR PRETTY LITTLE FRIEND ACQUIRES A SECOND SMILE.

SHE'S NAE FRIEND TEH ME.

CLATTER

WELCOME ABOARD, LADIES.

SOON, WE SAIL FOR THE DISTANT SHORES OF KHARTOUM.

A PRINCESS OF BLOOD ROYAL FETCHES QUITE A PRIZE IN THE EAST. IF YOU KNOW THE RIGHT BUYER.
WHA' ABOUT YER RANSOM?

WHAT RANSOM?

YEH LEFT THA' NOTE...
TO DELAY PURSUIT. YOU WERE THE ONLY ONE TOO SIMPLE TO BE FOOLED.

GENTLEMEN, CAST OFF. BY SUNSET, THIS LAND WILL ONLY BE A MEMORY.

I'M SURPRISED YER MEN HAVEN'T SORTED ME OUT, AFTER WHAT I DONE TEH 'EM.
THEY DO AS THEY'RE TOLD.
MEN LIKE THOSE CAN BE FOUND IN ANY CHEAP ALEHOUSE OR PRISON ACROSS THE FIVE KINGDOMS. THEY'RE SLAVES, EVER SEEKING A MASTER.
JUST LIKE THESE GIRLS HERE. AND ALL WHO CALL THEMSELVES "CIVILIZED."

THEY DARE NOT DREAM BOLD DREAMS, NOR WILL TO MAKE THEM TRUE.
ONCE I MAKE MY FORTUNE, I SHALL SAIL WHERE I WOULD, FREE FROM THE SHACKLES OF CIVILIZATION.

JUST DO AS YEH PLEASE, AN' TEH HELL WI' EVERYONE, EH?
IS THAT SCORN I DETECT? OR JEALOUSY?
BUT WHAT USE DO LAWS AND RULES OF CONDUCT HAVE FOR SUCH AS WE? WE WHO ARE STRONG OF LIMB AND WILL.

WHY NOT COME WITH ME?
YOU DON'T BELONG AMONG THOSE SIMPERING GIRLS, FETTERED BY LAWS THAT PROTECT THE WEAK FROM THE STRONG...

...THAT CALL US BARBARIANS, WE WHO SEE CIVILIZATION FOR WHAT IT IS...
...A PRISON.
COME WITH ME, AND BE FREE.
Think not less of your daughter, warchild of the mountains, for her moment of temptation.
For the cares of the world had long burdened her.
O, to rely on nought but her own steel and sinew, which have never failed her.
But presently she recalled the words of one whose steel and sinew outmatched all others.
ON THE DAY YEH FACE YER DEATH, ÜLGA, YEH'LL KNOW ONLY SERENITY.

'TIS HOPE MAKES A WARRIOR FEAR. WHEN YEH KNOW THAT IN YER HEART O' HEARTS...
...YEH'LL MAKE A FRIEND O' FEAR.
WHA' A PAIR O' COWARDS WE'D BE.
I FEAR NOTHING IN THIS WORLD!
YEH FEAR CIVILIZATION, WHERE STRENGTH ALONE IS NO' ENOUGH.
WHERE YEH MUST TRUST IN OTHERS, UNRELIABLE AS THEY MAY BE.

'TIS A THING YEH CANNAE DO.

SO HOW COULD WE TRUST EACH OTHER? WITHOUT CIVILIZATION, ALL MEN ARE ENEMIES.

AND ONLY A FOOL WOULD SLEEP BESIDE AN ENEMY.

ALAS, I MUST DECLINE YER OFFER.

I'LL TAKE ME CHANCES WI' CIVILIZATION...

...SUCH AS IT IS.

KILL THEM!

WHAT ARE YOU WAITING FOR? ATTACK!

ARE YOU JOKING? YOU SAW WHAT HAPPENED LAST TIME.

GOOD LUCK, CAPTAIN.
COWARDS!
YEH'LL NO' FIND MUCH LOYALTY WI' SLAVES, LAD. THERE'S NOTHIN' IN IT FOR 'EM.

YOU HAVEN'T SEEN THE LAST OF ME, PRINCESS.

YOU'RE FULL OF SURPRISES, AREN'T YOU?

I'D CERTAINLY BE SURPRISED TO FIND OUT SHE CAN SAIL.
WHICH IS TOO BAD, SINCE WE'RE GOING TO RUN AGROUND.

EVERYONE HOLD ONTO SOMETHING!

CRASH

NICE GOING, ÜLGA.
SHE SAVED OUR LIVES, JULIE. CAN'T YOU LET UP FOR A MOMENT?

AND HOW DO YOU SUPPOSE WE'LL GET HOME, PRAY TELL?
NO ONE WILL EVER FIND US HERE.

GOOD MORROW! WOULD YOUR HIGHNESSES CARE TO BE RESCUED?
NOT A MOMENT TOO SOON, GENTLEMEN.
YOU WERE SAYING?

OH, MALICK! I KNEW YOU'D COME FOR ME.
I TRIED TO STEER US CLEAR...

...BUT ALAS, WE WERE ALREADY GOING TOO FAST.
YEH DID FINE.
FER A LOWLANDER.

ÜLGA, WHAT ARE YOU DOING?
WHAT DOES IT LOOK LIKE?
ACCEPTIN' WHO I AM.

chapter 7

THE ROYAL AUDIENCE IS TOMORROW.

NO ONE EXPECTS YOU TO PARTICIPATE AFTER YOUR ORDEAL. BUT YOU'LL ALL HAVE A PLACE OF HONOR BESIDE HER MAJESTY.
WHAT DID WE COME HERE FOR? THE SHOW MUST GO ON.

I FEAR THIS SHOW ISN'AE GOIN' ANYWHERE.
THEN YOU SHOULD JUST GO BACK WHERE YOU CAME FROM.

YOU MEAN A REAL PRINCESS?
YOU DON'T BELONG HERE ANYWAY. YOU'RE NOT ONE OF US.

BECAUSE SHE DOESN'T SNEER AND PREEN AND TELL LIES AS WELL AS YOU? IS THAT ALL IT TAKES?
WHO DO YOU THINK YOU ARE, TALKING TO ME LIKE THAT?

I KNOW WHO I AM. AND WHO YOU ARE, TOO. I LOOKED YOU UP IN DOCTOR GAMOOSH'S PEERAGE BOOKS.
YOU KEEP GOING ON ABOUT NOBILITY AND BREEDING. I WANTED TO KNOW JUST HOW NOBLE YOU WERE.

IT TURNS OUT YOUR GRANDFATHER WAS A SUCCESSFUL PIG MERCHANT. AND YOUR MOTHER'S FAMILY WERE MONEYLENDERS. YOU'VE GOT LESS NOBLE BLOOD THAN MY BUTLER.

PRINCESS UGG'S ANCESTORS ONCE RULED ALL FIVE KINGDOMS. SHE'S MORE ROYAL THAN ANY OF US.

BUT YOU ALL SAW HER IN THAT CAVE, CHOPPING PEOPLE TO BITS!
SHE'S A MONSTER!
MAYBE SO, BUT SHE'S *OUR* MONSTER.
YOU THINK THAT STUPID HAT MAKES YOU A BETTER PRINCESS? IT'S NOT SOMETHING YOU WEAR, JULIE.

AND IF YOU'RE INCAPABLE OF GRATITUDE OR FRIENDSHIP, AT LEAST PRETEND YOU HAVE ENOUGH GOOD BREEDING TO BE CIVIL.

IF YOU CAN'T DO THAT, JUST SHUT UP.

MAL, WE NEED TO TALK.
JUST LET ME FINISH THIS REPORT TO YOUR FATHER. HE'D WANT TO KNOW THAT YOU'RE SAFE.

IT'S ABOUT THAT KISS. YOU KNOW, FROM PRINCESS UGG.
WHY MUST YOU INSIST ON CALLING HER THAT? IT'S NOT VERY GRACIOUS.

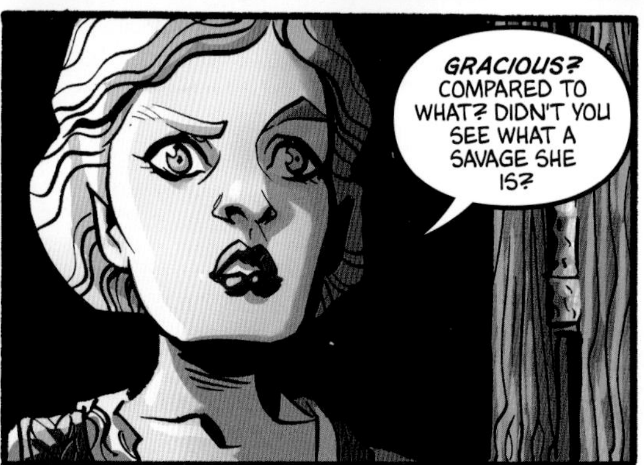
GRACIOUS? COMPARED TO WHAT? DIDN'T YOU SEE WHAT A SAVAGE SHE IS?

I SAW A VALIANT WARRIOR SAVING YOUR LIFE.

BUT YOU MUST ADMIT SHE'S NO LADY.
JULIE, I KNOW YOU HAVE A HARD TIME UNDERSTANDING THIS, BUT IT'S POSSIBLE TO BE BOTH A LADY *AND* VALIANT.

SO THAT'S HOW IT IS? EVEN YOU TURN YOUR BACK ON MY FRIENDSHIP?
YOU HAVE TO *BE* A FRIEND TO HAVE ONE, PRINCESS.

I GUESS YOU'VE FORGOTTEN WHAT MY FRIENDSHIP HAS GIVEN YOU, "CAPTAIN." NOT TO MENTION MY FATHER'S.

NOT EVEN TWENTY, AND CAPTAIN OF THE PRIME MINISTER'S GUARD. NOT BAD FOR THE THIRD SON OF A COUNTRY SQUIRE.

YOU HAVE NO IDEA HOW HARD I WORKED-
NOW HANG ON A MINUTE!
IMAGINE IF I WERE TO WITHDRAW MY "FRIENDSHIP." WHERE WOULD YOU BE THEN? YOU KNOW HOW FATHER DOTES ON ME.

OH, I KNOW EXACTLY WHAT YOU'VE DONE TO "SECURE YOUR POSITION." JUST REMEMBER IT MIGHT ALL HAVE BEEN FOR NOTHING.

IF I CAN BE SO EASILY CAST ASIDE, SO CAN YOU.
JULIE, PLEASE-
SLAM

THANK YOU, LADY JULIFER, FOR SUCH A REMARKABLE DISPLAY OF EQUESTRIAN SKILL.
COME CLOSER, MY CHILD.

PRINCESS JASMIN PERFORMS HER PEOPLE'S TRADITIONAL DANCE OF FERTILITY.

SHE'S NOT THE LAST ONE, IS SHE? I THOUGHT THERE WERE MORE GIRLS.

EVERY YEAR, THESE VISITS SEEM A LITTLE SHORTER.

I'M A'FEAR'D I SMASHED ME LUTE OVER SOME THIEVIN' KNACKER'S NOGGIN... ERR, YER MAJESTY.
THANK GOODNESS. I'VE HEARD ENOUGH OF THAT TUNE FOR THREE LIFETIMES.

BUT THEY SAY GRIMMERIAN MAIDENS SING LIKE ANGELS.
THEY DO?

ER, WELL, AYE, YER MAJESTY...
I S'POSE I CAN RECALL AN OLD LULLABY WE SING TEH OUR BABBIES. "ME BONNY FIGHTER."

'TIS NO' FANCY FOR A GREAT HALL SUCH AS THIS....
...BUT IT'S OURS.

AS SUN RETURNED FROM LANDS UNKNOWN
AN' GLIMMERED ON THE WATER
THA' YESTEREVE' WERE ICE AND SNOW,
A COMELY MOUNTAIN DAUGHTER

DID YOU KNOW SHE COULD SING LIKE THAT?
UH-UH!
I... I'VE NEVER HEARD ANYTHING LIKE IT.
GAVE HER SWEETHEART HAND AND HEART,
AN' TOOK HIM AS HER LOVER,
FOR SHE HAD KNOWN HIM ALL HER LIFE,
AN' THERE NAE COULD BE ANOTHER.
BUT PASSION MINGLED WI' REGRET,
AN' TEARS FELL ON HER SHOULDER,
FOR BITTER WAR BLOOMED WI' THE SPRING,
AN' NAE MORE COULD HE HOLD HER.
AN' AS HE KISSED HER ONE LAST TIME,
SHE HELD HIM EVER TIGHTER,
"PROMISE ME YEH SHALL RETURN,
O ME BONNY FIGHTER."
SPRING GAVE WAY TEH SUMMER SWEET,
AN' PURPLE WAS THE HEATHER
THA' SPILLED ACROSS THE HIGHLAND PEAKS,
A BED AS SOFT AS FEATHERS.

THOUGH GENTLE WAS THE SUN'S CARESS,
ITS WARMTH COULD NO' DELIGHT HER,
FOR THOUGH HIS SOLEMN WORD HE GAVE,
WAR CLAIMED HER BONNY FIGHTER.
RED LEAVES FELL, AND SOON HER HEART
WAS FILLED ANEW WI' RAPTURE.
THEIR LOVE BROUGHT FORTH A FINE STRONG SON,
WHOSE COUNTENANCE DID CAPTURE
THE FACE O' HIM FOR WHOM SHE PINED,
AN' MADE HER SORROW LIGHTER.
"SAY YEH WILLNAE GO TO WAR,
ME BONNY LITTLE FIGHTER."
THROUGH WINTER SNOWS AN' SUMMERS SWEET,
HE FILLED HER HEART WI' GLADNESS,
BUT AS HER BOY BECAME A MAN,
SO RETURNED HER SADNESS.
ONE GRIM SPRING MORN THE GIANTS CAME,
THE COLD BLUE-EYED INCITERS,
AN' BATTLE TORE HIM FROM HER ARMS...

HER YOUNG AN' BONNY FIGHTER.

ARE YOU AILING, YOUR MAJESTY? CAN I GET YOU ANYTHING?

OH, MY DEAR CHILD. YOU'VE NEVER KNOWN LOSS, HAVE YOU?
YOUR MAJESTY?

YOU WILL, ONE DAY.
AND THEN YOU'LL UNDERSTAND YOUR FRIEND'S SONG.

I CAN'T BELIEVE SHE GAVE YOU THAT.

WHY? WHA' IS IT?
ONLY THE DIADEM OF THE PRINCESSES OF ATRAESCA. THE CROWN JEWELS!

AYE, WELL, I'LL TRADE YEH FOR THAT WEE CLUB.

WHA'EVER IT IS, I RECKON IT'D PACK A MEAN WALLOP.
IT'S A SCEPTER.

THAT'S NOT WHAT IT'S FOR.
AYE, WELL, SHE SAID SHE'D NAE MORE USE FOR ANY O' IT.
HER CHILDREN ALL DIED, YOU KNOW.
SHE'S THE LAST QUEEN.

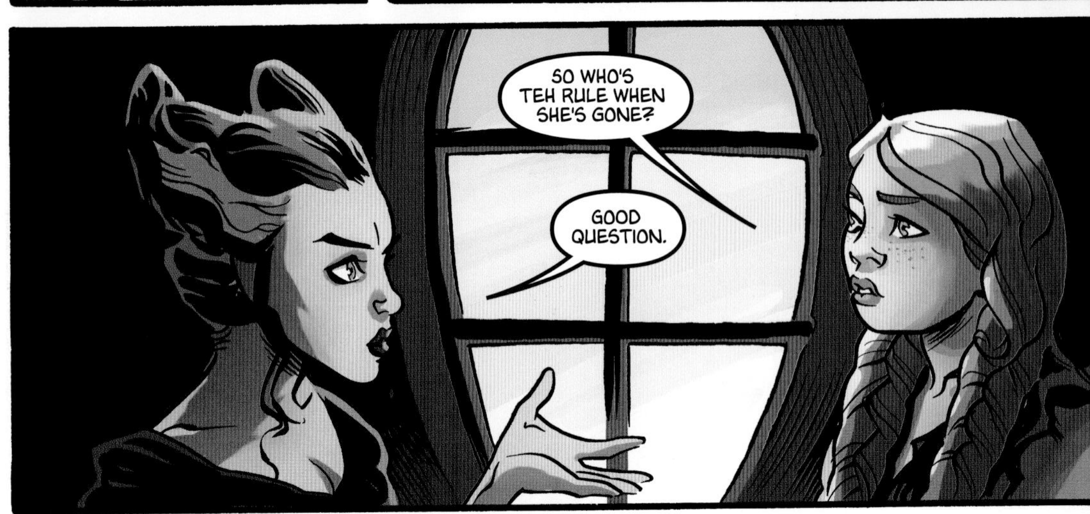
SO WHO'S TEH RULE WHEN SHE'S GONE?
GOOD QUESTION.

WE CAN
TAKE IT FROM
HERE. MANY
THANKS.

THIS
ISN'AE THE
ACADEMY.
WHERE ARE
WE GOIN'?

IT WON'T
TAKE LONG. THE PRIME
MINISTER WISHES TO SPEAK
WITH YOU ABOUT YOUR
ABDUCTION.
CAN'T HE
COME TO THE
SCHOOL?
I DINNAE
LIKE THE AIR IN THIS
PLACE. CAN WE OPEN
THE WINDOW?

YOU DON'T KNOW HIM LIKE I DO. HE CAN BARELY BE BOTHERED TO COME HOME ON WEEKENDS.
ACTUALLY, LADY JULIFER, HE'D LIKE TO SEE YOU RIGHT AWAY.

ME? WHY?
IS IT SO STRANGE THAT A FATHER IS CONCERNED FOR HIS DAUGHTER'S WELL BEING?

THAT DEPENDS ON THE FATHER.
DINNAE CLOSE THE DOOR. I'D LIKE TEH HAVE A WEE-

-TINKLE...
K-CHUNK

GREAT YOG! ARE WE IN THE... DUNGEON?

DO YOU HAVE ANY IDEA HOW MANY TREATIES YOU'RE BREAKING?
THESE ARE OUR ALLIES!
DECADES OF FRIENDLY COEXISTENCE...
IT'S NO USE FUSSING LIKE OLD WIVES NOW. IT'S DONE.
BUT WHY?

QUEEN ASTORIA'S LINE DIES WITH HER.
SHE'S BEEN HAPPY ENOUGH TO LEAVE GOVERNMENT TO THE GOVERNORS.
BUT HER SUCCESSOR MAY NOT BE SO FORWARD-THINKING.

AND WHAT DO YOU PROPOSE?
AS YOU KNOW, ROYALTY INTERBREEDS LIKE RABBITS IN A WARREN. ANY OF A DOZEN SCIONS MAY CLAIM RIGHTFUL SUCCESSION, GENTLEMEN.
IT'S NOT JUST OUR POSITIONS WE STAND TO LOSE, SHOULD THE CROWN PASS TO THE WRONG PERSON.

THE YOUNG LADIES WILL REMAIN OUR "GUESTS" TO ENSURE CONTINUED FRIENDLINESS BETWEEN COUNTRIES. AND WHO KNOWS?

LOVE BLOSSOMS IN THE STRANGEST CIRCUMSTANCES.
I'M SURE NONE OF US WOULD OBJECT TO MARRYING INTO A KINGDOM.

YOU PLAY A DANGEROUS GAME, SIR.

I'M SO GLAD WE'RE ALL IN AGREEMENT.
NOW IF YOU'LL EXCUSE ME, I MUST PREPARE FOR THE AMBASSADORS' ARRIVAL.

OH, HELLO, MY DEAR. WHAT ARE YOU DOING HERE?
WELL, ALL MY FRIENDS ARE IN THE DUNGEON, YOU SEE.

I GOT THE IDEA FROM YOUR YOUNG CAPTAIN FRIEND. HE THOUGHT THOSE BANDITS HAD A SURPRISINGLY CLEVER LITTLE PLAN. I AGREE.
DON'T WORRY, MY TREASURE. YOUR FRIENDS WILL COME TO NO HARM.

BESIDES, YOU ALWAYS COMPLAINED THAT YOU WEREN'T A TRUE PRINCESS LIKE THE REST.
YEAH. PHOE WAS NICE ENOUGH TO REMIND ME.

WELL, SOON YOU'LL BE THE DAUGHTER OF AN EMPEROR.
THIS IS JUST THE BEGINNING.

I'M WORRIED ABOUT JULIFER. SHE MIGHTA GOTTEN HERSELF INTO WORSE TROUBLE THAN US. YEH KNOW HOW SHE IS WITH THAT MOUTH.

ÜLGA, WHO DO YOU THINK PUT US HERE?

I DINNAE KNOW.
JULIE'S FATHER, THE PRIME MINISTER, THAT'S WHO. MY MOM SAID HE WAS THE CROOKEDEST MAN SHE EVER MET.

HE RATHER IMPRESSED HER, ACTUALLY.
WHEREVER JULIFER IS, SHE'S NOT IN ANY TROUBLE. SHE HUNG US OUT TO DRY.

WHY DOES SHE HATE ME SO? I ONLY TRIED TEH BE HER FRIEND.

PEOPLE LIKE HER AREN'T CAPABLE OF FRIENDSHIP. ALL THEY CARE ABOUT IS HOW TO GET AHEAD.

YOU DON'T LOOK HAPPY, MY DEAR.

SMILE. YOU'RE GETTING EVERYTHING YOU WANT, AS USUAL.
AND YOU? WHAT DO YOU GET OUT OF IT? IT SEEMS YOU DON'T NEED ME ANYMORE.

A STAKE IN THE NEW EMPIRE, OF COURSE. AND PERHAPS EVEN A ROYAL MARRIAGE.
I SUPPOSE ÜLGA LIKES YOU.

THANK YOU, GENTLEMEN. I'M SURE EVERYTHING WILL WORK OUT TO OUR MUTUAL SATISFACTION.

IS THAT EVERYONE?
THERE'S STILL THE *ehem* DELEGATION FROM GRIMMERIA.

THEY ARE THE KEY TO OUR MILITARY STRATEGY, YOUR EXCELLENCY.
AH. WHAT DO WE WANT FROM THEM AGAIN?

GRIMMERIAN STEEL. IT CUTS ORDINARY STEEL LIKE BUTTER.
UNDER THE RIGHT LEADERSHIP, A THOUSAND GRIMMERIAN SOLDIERS COULD CONQUER ANY ARMY IN THE WORLD.

THE DELEGATION FROM GRIMMERIA.

I'D LIKE TO START BY SAYING THAT I ONLY DESIRE FRIENDSHIP BETWEEN OUR KINGDOMS.
A MILITARY ALLIANCE WILL BUILD GOOD FAITH, HELP US LEARN ABOUT EACH OTHER, AND FOSTER UNDERSTANDING BETWEEN OUR LANDS.

SO YEH WANT OUR SWORDS, THEN?

YEH CAN HA' THIS ONE!

SHWAP

THUNK
THUNK
THUNK

TRY YOUR SKILL AGAINST ME, OLD MAN! I'VE DEFEATED EVERY KNIGHT IN THIS KINGDOM.
HAVE YEH, NOW?
KLANK

WAK
DID THEY GET HIM?
HE ESCAPED.
cough
SIR, I DON'T KNOW HOW WELL YOU KNOW YOUR HISTORY, BUT THE LAST TIME THIS CITY WENT TO WAR WITH THE MOUNTAIN BARBARIANS–
THEY HAVE STEEL.
BUT WORDS CAN SOMETIMES LEAVE DEEPER WOUNDS.

chapter 8

TOMORROW, WE TACK BACK OOR LANDS, OR DIE TRYIN'!
DEATH TUH THE BLOODHEADS!!!
THEY'RE MASSIN'. T'WILL NAE BE LONG.
IF THEY BREAK THROUGH TEH THE FERTILE DELLS, THEY'LL GAIN THE ADVANTAGE.
AT ALL COSTS, WE MUST NAE-
TEH ME, WARRIORS O' GRIMMERIA!

KING THORGRIM! JUST IN TIME. WE ATTACK AT–
GATHER YER GEAR! WE MUST REACH THE VALLEY BY SUNSET TOMORROW!
WHAT?!

BUT THE GIANTS! WE CANNAE ALLOW THEM ACCESS TEH OUR DELLS–
TEH HELL WI' THE DELLS. THEY CAN 'AVE 'EM!

HAVE YEH GONE MAD? WE CANNAE–

IT SEEMS ALL YOUR KINGDOMS HAVE SEEN REASON.
EXCEPT YOURS, ÜLGA. YOUR FATHER DOESN'T APPRECIATE THE GRAVITY OF YOUR SITUATION.
SHACKLE HER.
CLICK

RIGHT, YEH KNACKER. LET'S SORT YEH OUT FIRST!
CLUNK

I THINK NOT.
THUNK

ALL THAT STRENGTH, DEFEATED BY A SIMPLE MECHANICAL DEVICE.
SUDDENLY, I'M NOT SO WORRIED ABOUT YOUR FATHER'S THREATS.

I'M SORRY, ÜLGA. BUT MY MASTER WANTS TO SEND A CLEAR MESSAGE.
LAY HER ARM FLAT.

I THINK THAT HAND HAS DONE ENOUGH DAMAGE.

MAYBE WITHOUT IT, YOU'LL LEARN TO BE A PROPER LADY.

OOOOOWW!

JULIE? WHAT DO YOU THINK YOU'RE DOING?

OPENING MY EYES.

I TOLD YEH THAT'D MAKE A BONNY CLUB.
MILADY, WHAT IS ALL THIS?

HOLD! WE CANNOT LET YOU PASS.
err... YOUR HIGHNESSES.

RAAAAAAAAAAH!!!
GRAAAAAAAAAAAWWWLL!!!
AAAAAAAAAAAAAH!!

YOU'RE NOT GOING ANYWHERE, PRINCESS!

GRIMMERIAN STEEL. HARD AS DIAMOND. IT'LL CUT THROUGH THAT BLADE LIKE BUTTER.
ONE THING ME MITHER TAUGHT ME ABOUT THE FLINT BLADES O' THE STONE GIANTS...
IF YEH'RE TOO HARD...
...YEH'RE EASILY SHATTERED.

ANY MORE BRIGHT IDEAS, JULIE?

ACTUALLY, YEAH.

RAAAAAAAAGH!!!!

WHAT'S GOING ON OUT HERE?
THANK EYDÍS FOR FRESH AIR.
BALDUR'S BEARD!
'TIS ME FATHER!

I APPRECIATE YOUR HIGH SPIRITS, BUT YOU MUST LOOK AT THIS LOGICALLY.

WE HAVE HIGH WALLS, LONGBOWS AND CATAPULTS.
NOT TO MENTION THE FULL MILITARY SUPPORT OF OUR ALLIES.

THINK OF THE COST OF SUCH A SIEGE, IN TIME, IN LIVES...

WE DINNAE FEAR DEATH. WE'LL FIGHT TEH THE LAST MAN!

AND THEN YOUR WIVES AND CHILDREN WOULD BE DEFENSELESS.
YEH DINNAE KNOW OUR WIVES.
AND IN THE MEANTIME, YOU'LL HAVE FORFEITED YOUR DAUGHTER'S LIFE.

I WILLNAE JUST ROLL OVER.

CONSIDER WHAT YOU HAVE TO LOSE.
A LITTLE PRIDE...

...COMPARED WITH THE LIVES OF YOUR DAUGHTER AND HUNDREDS OF YOUR PEOPLE?
IT'S NOT A DIFFICULT CALCULATION.

I'M SORRY, DAUGHTER...

I CANNAE SEE A BETTER WAY.
FATHER?

ARE YEH WEEPIN'?

ÜLGA?

I THOUGHT I'D LOST YEH, ME BONNY WEE BERZERKER.
I'M FINE, DA.

EVERYTHIN'S GOIN' TEH BE FINE.

THAT DIDN'T TAKE LONG.
AYE, WELL, I'M NO' MUCH OF A THINKER.

WHICH IS WHY I JUST ELECTED A NEGOTIATOR.

AN' YEH MAY HA' TEH FORGIVE HER INEXPERIENCE...

...BUT SHE SEEMS TEH HA' A DIFFERENT VIEW OF OUR SITUATION.
GREAT ALBION! HOW-?

MY LORD! THE PRINCESSES! THEY'VE ESCAPED! I-

Oh.

WHAT OUR FRIEND WAS ABOUT TEH EXPLAIN BEFORE HE LOST HIS TONGUE WAS THA' THE PRINCESSES ARE NAE LONGER YER PRISONERS.

THEY'RE *MY* PRISONERS NOW.
AND I HA' A LIST O' DEMANDS FOR THEIR SAFE RETURN.

MY FRIENDS, WE CAN'T LET THIS *BARBARIAN* DICTATE TERMS TO US!
HOW DARE YOU?
WHY NOT? *YOU* DID.
THAT WAS SIMPLY POLITICS. I'M A CIVILIZED MAN.

AND WHEN YEH SENT YER BOY DOWN TEH CUT ME HAND OFF? WAS THAT POLITICS TOO?

I'M NOT GOING TO SIT HERE AND LISTEN TO THESE LIES. GENTLEMEN?
WHAT ABOUT OUR DAUGHTERS?

A REGRETTABLE LOSS, BUT CLEARLY THERE'S NO TREATING WITH THESE... *ANIMALS!*
THIS IS WAR NOW, I'M AFRAID.
WHA' ABOUT JULIFER?

IS SHE TEH BE A REGRETTABLE LOSS TOO?
YOU'RE BLUFFING.
WALK OUT THA' DOOR AND YEH'LL NEVER SEE HER AGAIN.
YOU WOULDN'T DARE!

TRY ME.

RAAAAAAAAAAH!
HOLD HIM!
YOU LITTLE MONSTER! I'LL HAVE YOU BURNED ALIVE!

IT APPEARS WE HAVE NO CHOICE BUT TO HEAR YOUR DEMANDS.
GET HIM OUT OF HERE.

BUT CONSIDER CAREFULLY, PRINCESS. YOU HOLD THE FATE OF MANY KINGDOMS IN YOUR HANDS, INCLUDING YOUR OWN.

AYE, WELL, I'M NAE DIPLOMAT LIKE YEH LOT, SO I'LL KEEP IT SIMPLE.

EACH O' YER KINGDOMS MUST BRING FORTH ITS MOST PRECIOUS TREASURE AS TRIBUTE.

I'M SPEAKIN' O' COURSE, O' THE SILVER...
...IN YER TONGUES.

I NEED YER BEST AND BRIGHTEST DIPLOMATS.
IF YEH CAN SETTLE THIS MESS TEH EVERYONE'S SATISFACTION WI'OUT RESORTIN' TEH BLOODSHED, YEH'LL GET YER PRECIOUS PRINCESSES BACK.

IN THE MEANTIME, THEY'RE COMIN' TEH THE MOUNTAINS WI' US.
YOU'RE STEALING THEM AWAY TO THAT ICY HELL?
NO, UNCLE.

WE'RE GOING ON VACATION TILL YOU WISE OLD MEN QUIT ACTING LIKE A BUNCH OF...
BARBARIANS.
THANK YOU, JULIE. WELL PUT.

SHE LIES YONDER.
WHERE YON WEE FLOWERS ARE GROWIN'.
AND I THOUGHT MY PALACE WAS GRAND.
DO YOU MISS HER?
EVERY DAY.
I WISH I REMEMBERED MINE.

..UH, ÜLGA?

ARE THEY FRIENDS OF YOURS?

YOU KEEP YOUR DISTANCE!

THAT'S RIGHT! RESPECT THE SCEPTER.

HAIL! I AM ÜLGA, DAUGHTER O' QUEEN FRIÐRIKA.
AN' I HA' A MESSAGE FOR YER KING.
OOR KING BE DEID.
YUH TOOK OOR KINE AN' OOR LANDS! WHAT MOOR D'YUH WANT OF OOS?
STRANGE AS IT MAY SOUND, I WANT FRIENDSHIP.

ORE YUH JOOKIN'?
FOR NOW I'LL SETTLE FOR CIVILIZED CONVERSATION.

YUH THINK AFTER WUT YUH DOON, WE'LL JUST COME OOT AND TALK?

WE COULD GO ON FIGHTIN', I S'POSE.
BUT YER BABBIES ARE STARVIN, YER MITHERS ARE GRIEVIN'...

...AN' SO 'RE OURS.

WE CAN RETURN YER LIVESTOCK AN' HELP YEH THROUGH THE SPRING.
AS FER THE LANDS WE BEEN FIGHTIN' OVER ALL THESE YEARS, PERHAPS WE COULD SHARE 'EM.
BUT IF ANY O' THAT'S TEH HAPPEN, WE MUST STOP FIGHTIN' AN' START TALKIN'.
I DUNNO WHY, GIRL, BUT YUH SCARES I MORE 'N ANY BLOODHEAD I EVER MET.

'TIS BECAUSE I'M OFFERIN' HOPE.
DID YER MITHER NEVER TELL YEH?
'TIS HOPE MAKES YEH FEAR.

Ted Naifeh's

PRINCESS UGG

COVER
&
PINUP
GALLERY

Issue #5: Retail Edition

Cover for Princess Ugg #5 illustrated and colored by Ted Naifeh

Issue #6: Retail Edition

Cover for Princess Ugg #6 illustrated and colored by Ted Naifeh

Issue #7: Retail Edition

Cover for Princess Ugg #7 illustrated and colored by Ted Naifeh

Issue #8: Retail Edition

Cover for Princess Ugg #8 illustrated and colored by Ted Naifeh

Pinup by

TERRY BLAS

‡

@TerryBlas · terryblas.com

Pinup by

WARREN WUCINICH

‡

@warrenwucinich · warrenwucinich.carbonmade.com

Pinup by

EMILY C. MARTIN

‡

@megamoth · megamoth.net

Pinup by

EMILY C. MARTIN

‡

@megamoth · megamoth.net

ted naifeh

Ted Naifeh has been creating successful independent comics since the late 90s. He co-created ***Gloomcookie***, the goth romance comic, with author Serena Valentino, and soon after began writing and drawing ***Courtney Crumrin and the Night Things***, a spooky children's fantasy series about a grumpy little girl and her adventures with her Warlock uncle.

Nominated for an Eisner Award for best limited series, ***Courtney Crumrin's*** success paved the way for ***Polly and the Pirates***, this time about a prim and proper girl kidnapped by pirates who believe her to be the daughter of their long-lost queen. ***Courtney Crumrin*** now has six volumes, plus a spin-off book, and ***Polly and the Pirates*** has two.

Ted also co-created ***How Loathsome*** with Tristan Crane, and illustrated two volumes of ***Death Junior*** with screenwriter Gary Whitta. More recently, he illustrated ***The Good Neighbors***, a three-volume graphic novel series written by New York Times best-selling author Holly Black, published by Scholastic.

Recently, Ted has contributed work to many major comics companies, including ***Batman*** comics for DC, and the horror anthology ***Creepy*** for Dark Horse.

warren wucinich

Warren Wucinich has worked as a professional illustrator and cartoonist since 1999. Serving as either illustrator, colorist or letterer, Warren has worked on several Oni Press titles including ***Courtney Crumrin, Jam! Tales From the World of Roller Derby, Rascal Raccoon's Raging Revenge!, Resurrection*** and ***Spell Checkers*** among others.

Warren has also published works through Image, Pop! Goes the Icon and Poseur Ink. He currently resides in Durham, NC where he spends most of his time making comics, watching *Star Trek* reruns and complaining about mosquitoes.